.50

Withdrawn

ASK A SILLY QUESTION

By Joyce Wakefield

Illustrated by Mike Venezia

 CHILDRENS PRESS, CHICAGO

Wakefield, Joyce.
  Ask a silly question.

  SUMMARY: Presents riddles such as "What's the
difference between your left shoe and a pot of glue?
You can wear the pot of glue on either foot."
  1. Riddles—Juvenile literature. [1. Riddles]
I. Venezia, Mike. II. Title.
PN6371.5.W3   398.6   78-24248
ISBN 0-516-03408-1

2 3 4 5 6 7 8 9 10 11 12 R 85 84 83 82 81 80 79

What's the difference
between . . .

a **lamb** and a **jar of jam?**

Jam goes better with peanut butter.

What's the difference
between . . .

your left shoe and a **pot of glue?**

You can wear the pot of glue
on either foot.

What's the difference between . . .

an **alligator** and an **elevator?**

If you get in an alligator,
you can't
get off on the 10th floor.

What's the difference
between . . .

a **wig** and a **pig?**

A pig eats more.

What's the difference
between . . .

a **cookie jar** and a **movie star?**

It's hard to keep your money
in a movie star.

What's the difference
between . . .

a **nickle** and a **pickle**?

If you put a pickle in a parking
meter, you'll get a ticket.

What's the difference between . . .

a **duck** and a **truck?**

Who ever heard of a pickup duck?

What's the difference
between . . .

a **road** and a **toad?**

There aren't as many signs
on a toad.

What's the difference
between . . .

mice and **rice?**

It's not nice to throw mice
at a wedding.

What's the difference
between . . . .

a **bumble bee** and a **Christmas tree?**

If you trim a bumble bee
it might sting you.

What's the difference
between . . .

an **ape** and a **drape?**

23

If an ape hangs on your window, you
have to keep feeding it bananas.

What's the difference
between . . .

a **park** and a **shark?**

A shark doesn't have drinking fountains.

What's the difference
between . . .

a **postcard** and a **St. Bernard?**

It takes more stamps to mail
a Saint Bernard.

What's the difference
between . . .

a **flea** and a **ski?**

If you can slide down a hill
on two fleas, you may be the
world's best skier.

What's the difference
between . . .

a **garter snake** and a **chocolate shake?**

The garter snake gets stuck
in your straw.